THE GIANT Walt Disney WORD BOOK

THE GIANT Walt Disney WORD BOOK

GOLDEN PRESS · NEW YORK
Western Publishing Company, Inc.
Racine, Wisconsin

Copyright © 1971 Walt Disney Productions. World rights reserved. Printed in the U.S.A.
First published 1971 by Purnell, England. U.S. Edition published 1972 by Golden Press, New York, N. Y.
Library of Congress Catalog Card Number: 72-78621
GOLDEN, A GOLDEN BOOK® and GOLDEN PRESS® are trademarks of Western Publishing Company, Inc.

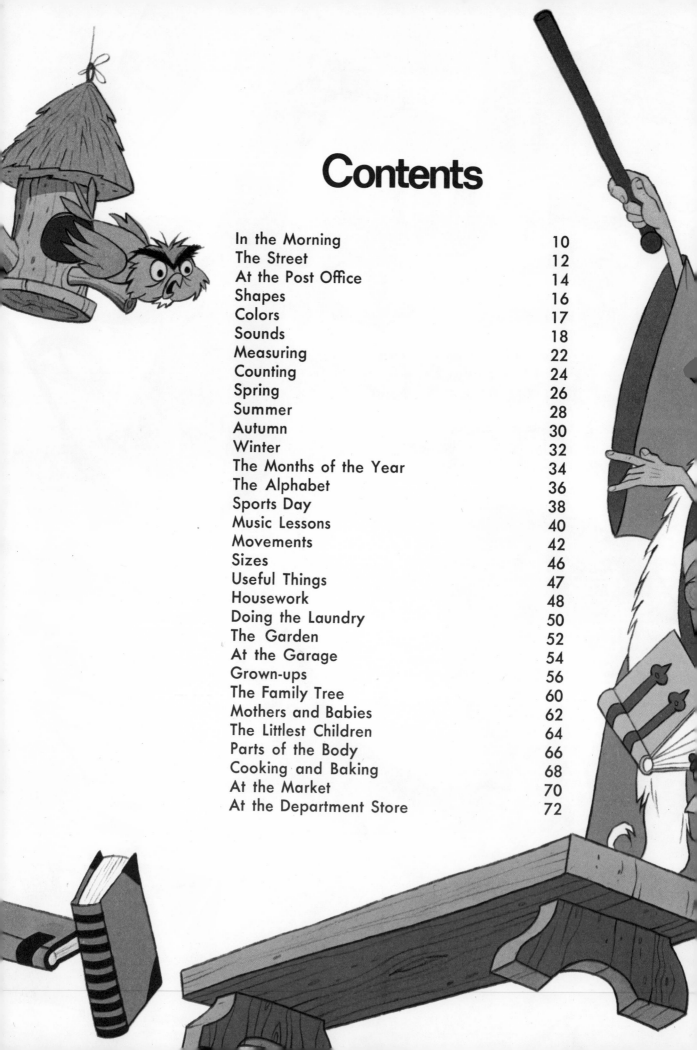

Contents

IN THE MORNING

Little Chipmunk has just awakened.
It is a lovely bright morning.

He gets up and washes and
dries himself.

curtain
pillow
sun
window
soapy face
bed
blanket

faucets
washbasin
towel

Now he brushes his teeth.

toothbrush
pajamas

He puts on his trousers.

underpants
undershirt
trousers

squashed ear
sweater

And he puts on his sweater.

hairbrush

mirror

stool

bureau

Little Chipmunk is ready for breakfast.

napkin

knife

spoon

plate fork

chair

table

He brushes his hair.

orange juice

milk

mother

toast

bacon and eggs

tray

Little Chipmunk and his mother have breakfast together.

coffeepot

cereal cream

coffee

His mother brings his breakfast. This is what she brings him.

When they have finished breakfast, Little Chipmunk helps his mother wash the dishes.

dish mop

saucepan

apron

dish-towel

11

THE STREET

change purse

shopping

milk truck

shopping basket

milkman

newspapers

milk bottles

newsboy

mailman

little dog

lamp post

trash basket

letters

litter basket

big dog

mailbag

scrap paper
(should be in the litter basket)

telephone booth

baby

ence

Mrs. Duck

baby carriage

helmet

sewer grating

policeman

leaf

notebook

delivery boy

packages
of meat

pencil

basket

bicycle

13

AT THE POST OFFICE

mailman

BUY SAVINGS BONDS

SEND A MONEY ORDER

bulletin board

mailbag

letters

sorting the letters

sending away for a dog license

LICENSE

mailbox

postmistress

grill

putting on the postmark

buying stamps

letter scale

14

money drawer

counter

money for stamps

piggy bank

mail truck

weighing a package

entering a contest

paying bills

receiving a package

pen

chain

sending
a postcard

writing counter

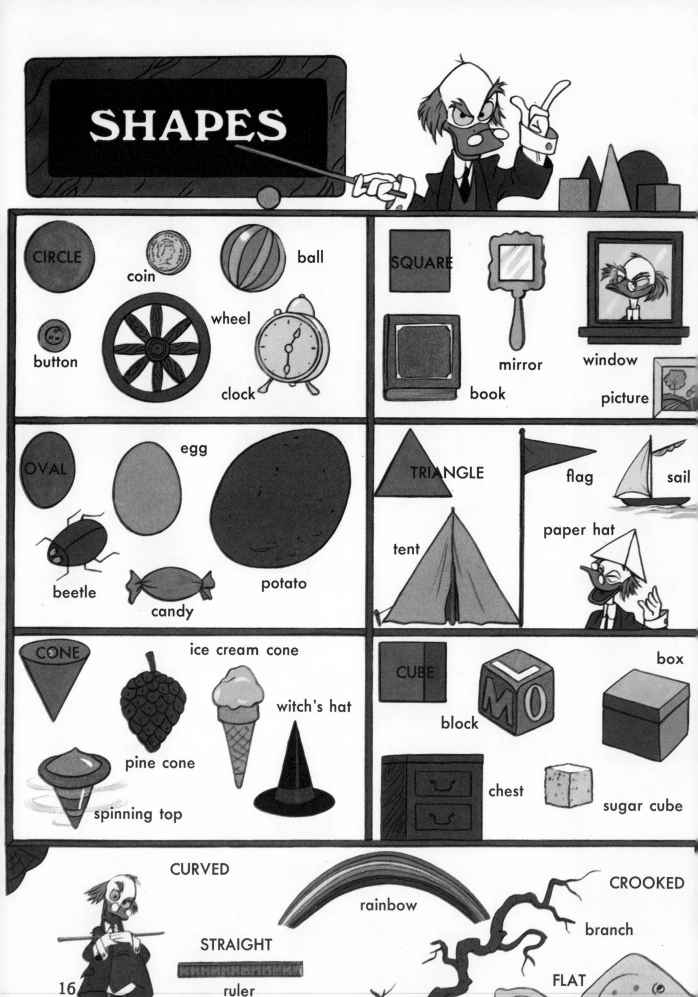

SHAPES

CIRCLE
coin
ball
button
wheel
clock

SQUARE
mirror
window
book
picture

OVAL
egg
beetle
candy
potato

TRIANGLE
flag
sail
tent
paper hat

CONE
ice cream cone
pine cone
witch's hat
spinning top

CUBE
box
block
chest
sugar cube

CURVED
rainbow

CROOKED
branch

STRAIGHT
ruler

FLAT
skate fish

16

COLORS

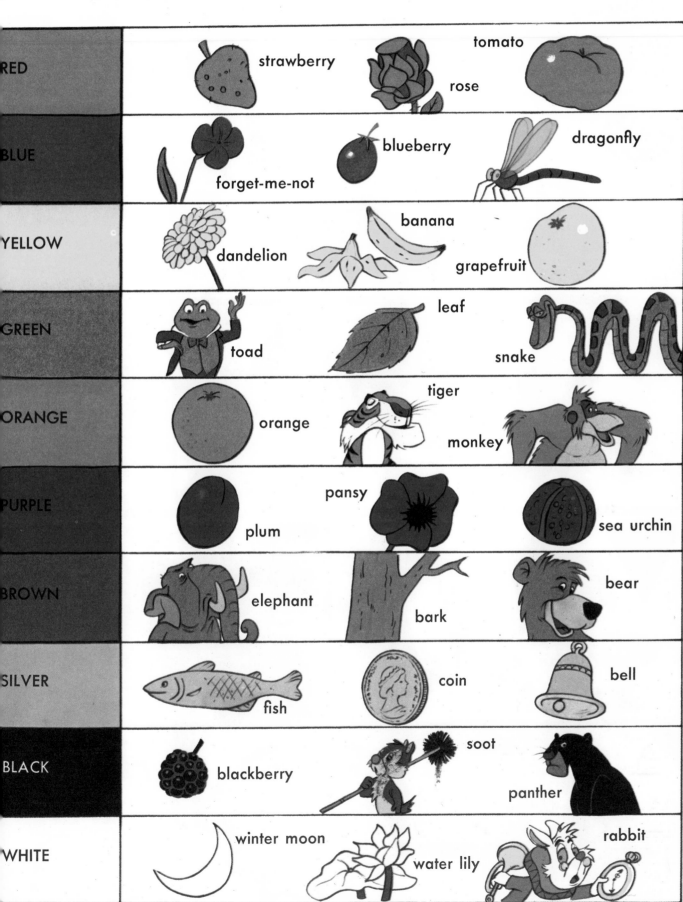

RED	strawberry, rose, tomato
BLUE	forget-me-not, blueberry, dragonfly
YELLOW	dandelion, banana, grapefruit
GREEN	toad, leaf, snake
ORANGE	orange, tiger, monkey
PURPLE	plum, pansy, sea urchin
BROWN	elephant, bark, bear
SILVER	fish, coin, bell
BLACK	blackberry, soot, panther
WHITE	winter moon, water lily, rabbit

SOUNDS

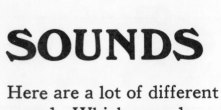

Here are a lot of different sounds. Which ones do you like best? Which is the loudest and which is the quietest? Which is the funniest?

BEE

buzz

HORSE

neigh

clip-clop

rustle

DEAD LEAVES

trring

BICYCLE BELL

slither-slither

OWL

tuwit-tuwooo

BELL

ding-dong

cheep

CHICKS

quack

DUCK

croak

SNAKE

FROG

19

moo

COW

HEN

cluck-cluck

oink

PIG

woof

DOG

meow

CAT

roar

LION

FIRECRACKER

ka-boom

caw

CROW

cock-a-doodle-doo

crackle

ICE

ROOSTER

hee-haw

DONKEY

pitter-patter

MOUSE

21

MEASURING

scale
(for weighing people)

kitchen scale

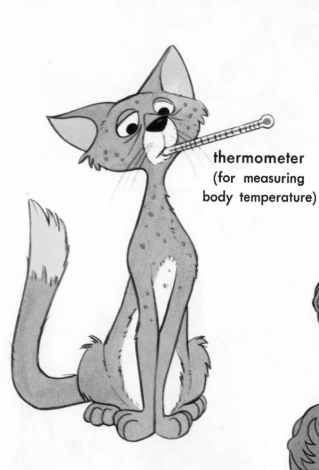

thermometer
(for measuring
body temperature)

barometer
(for measuring
air pressure)

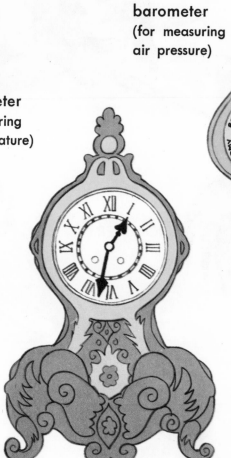

clock
(to tell time)

calendar

days

months

weeks

25

DECEMBER

WEEK 52

weather vane

measuring cup

trailer truck scale

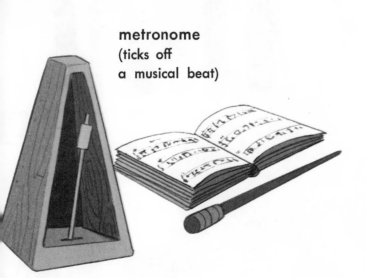

metronome
(ticks off
a musical beat)

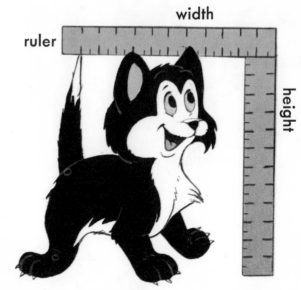

width

ruler

height

COUNTING

1 one lion

2 two cars

3 three bears

4 four shoes

5 five crows

6 six clocks

7 seven candles

24

8 eight mice

9   nine daisies

10   ten toy soldiers

11   eleven toadstools

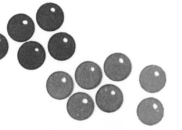

12   twelve marbles

13   thirteen minnows

14   fourteen thimbles

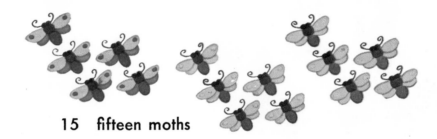

15   fifteen moths

16   sixteen sea horses

17   seventeen stars

18   eighteen thumbtacks

19   nineteen beans

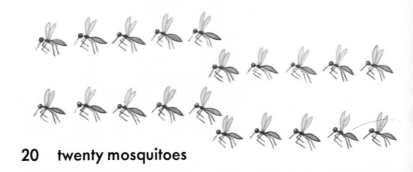

20   twenty mosquitoes

SPRING

willow buds

cloud

baby b

snowdrop

shower

crocus

lamb

sowing seeds

cuckoo

squirrel

robin

eggs

nest

daffodil

tree

buds

badger

tadpoles

mole

net

early bird

worm

SUMMER

lemonade

picnic hamper

wasp

sunbathing

soup flask

ice cream

strawberries

picnic cloth

dandelion

sun

butterfly

mole

sandwiches

busy bee

cake

pool

daisy

buttercup

29

preserves

swallows

haystack

AUTUMN

sheaf of wheat

farmer

smoke

falling leaves

flames

bonfire

horse chestnuts

squirrel

mole

nuts

31

cold ears

WINTER

frozen fingers

skis

numb toes

mole

ice skates

32

sled

snow

icicle

clearing a path

hot chestnuts

brazier

THE MONTHS OF THE YEAR

January: fun with snow

February: lots of mud

March: windy days

April: sudden showers

May: blooming flowers

June: sunny days

July: vacation time

August: harvest time

September: off to school

October: falling leaves

November: frosty nights

December: Christmas

THE ALPHABET

A armadillo

B bath

C crocodile

D donkey

E envelope

F frog

G gate

H house

I ibis

J jumper

K kangaroo (another kind of jumper)

L lion

M mouse

36

N net

O ostrich

P palace

Q queen

R royalty

S shell

T toadstool

U umbrella

V vole

W witch

X xylophone

Y yoyo

Z zipper

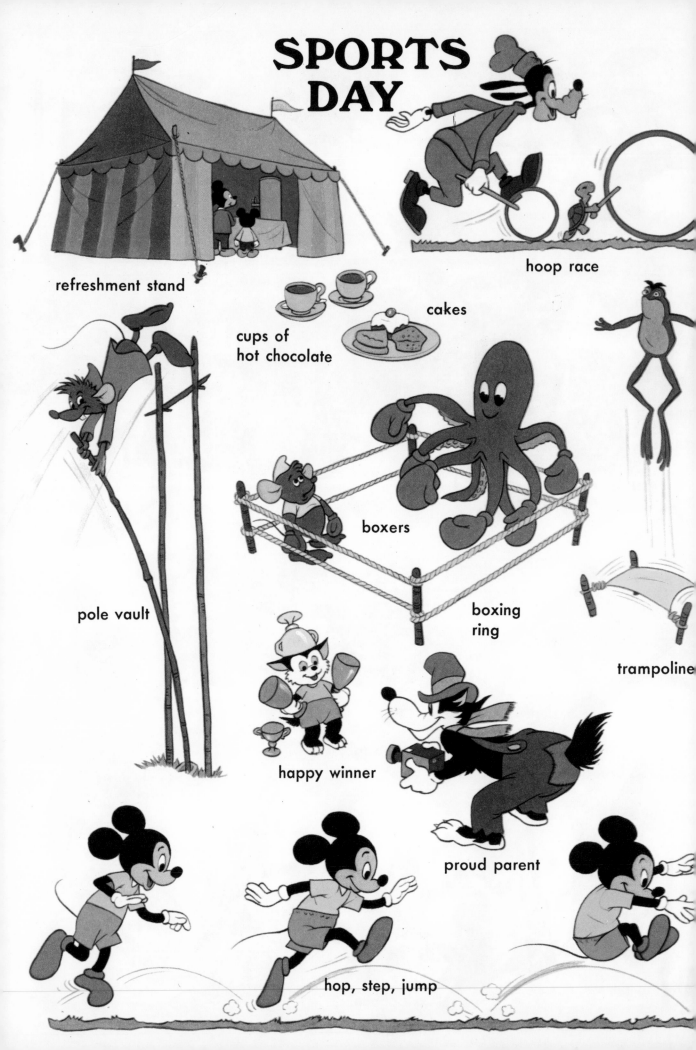

SPORTS DAY

refreshment stand

hoop race

cups of
hot chocolate

cakes

pole vault

boxers

boxing
ring

trampoline

happy winner

proud parent

hop, step, jump

egg and spoon race

dropped egg

sack race

high jump

obstacle race

broad jump

three-legged race

39

MUSIC LESSONS

harmonica

sweet music

saxophone

piano

cymba[l]

bassoon

trombone

double bass

piccolo

violin

clarinet

40

oboe

recorder

trumpet

wrong note

harp

French horn

triangle

kettle drum

singer

gong

bass drum

guitar

flute

cello

tuba

pipe organ

41

MOVEMENTS

crawl

sit

stand

lie down

skip

jump

hop

look up

look around

look down

walk

kneel

crouch

leap

bend over

43

dance

skate

twirl

float

dive

throw

catch

44

swing

run

pull

kick

vault

swim

45

SIZES

big

wide

tall

little

fat   thin

tiny

small

short

long

USEFUL THINGS

Toad turned out his pockets and here are all the useful things he found. How many things do you have in your pocket?

thumbtack

safety pin

key

pin

bean

raisin

lint

crumb

pebble

peanut

penknife

tape

bead

string

stamp

candy

paper clip

bus ticket

shell

thimble

marble

feather

blade of grass

empty spool

47

HOUSEWORK

soap bubbles

liquid detergent

messy cupboard

dirty dishes

bowl

plate rack

dirty old rubbish

wipe-up cloth

spilled cereal

trash can

broken chair

watering can

flower pot

hammer

can of polish

nails

glue

polishing cloth

48

feather duster

bucket

scrub brush

mop

dust

dirty footmarks

electrical outlet

plug

brush

crumbs

dustpan

broken plate

glue

cord

torn tablecloth

sewing machine

vacuum cleaner

49

DOING THE LAUNDRY

dirty sheets

dirty curtains

tub

kitten who doesn't like wash day

soaking clothes

soap powder

dirty towel

clothes hamper

(should be in the clothes hampe[r]

washing machine

ironing boa[rd]

iron

ironed sheets

drying rack

wrinkled sheet

clothes line

clothespins

socks

pole

sweater

undershirt

linen closet

laundry basket

needle

button

thread

children in clean clothes
How long do you think they will stay like this?

tired-out mother

51

THE GARDEN

apples

hedge clippers

apple tree

pitchfork

ladder

hedge

bee

rose

raspberries

honeycomb

hoe

spade

beehive

rake

peas

leaves

queen bee

greenhouse
(Don't kick a ball
when you're near one.)

gooseberry bush

potato patch

seedlings

lawn

lawnmower

lettuce
(tempting
for little rabbits)

iris

sprinkler

FERTILIZER   ERTILIZER

carrots

fertilizer

wer garden

basket

pansy

wheelbarrow

53

AT THE GARAGE

rack

tool bench

electric dri

hammer

mechanic

brace

nuts

car wash

OUT OF ORDER

grease

bolt

screwdriver

screw

wrench

jack

54

olish

polishing
cloth

car shampoo

gasoline tanker
(filling up the
garage's gas tank)

gasoline
pump

tire

air hose

sidelight

batteries

radiator

oil cans

headlight

windshield wipers

new tires

hood

trunk

GROWN-UPS

When you are grown-up you will have to decide what you want to do. Which job would you like best?

teacher

cook

dentist

author

astronaut

bus driver

mechanic

pianist

singer

57

artist

model

house painter

fireman

gardener

mountaineer

Mail

mailman

THE FAMILY TREE

great-great-grandfather

great-great-aunt

great-great-uncle

great-aunt

grandmother

grandfather

uncle

aunt

cousin

cousin

60

great-great-grandmother

great-grandfather

great-grandmother

great-uncle

grandfather

grandmother

father

mother

sister

brother

me

My name is Jimminy Cricket.

61

MOTHERS
AND BABIES

HORSE

CAT

kitten

foal

PIG

piglet

FROG

tadpole

cub

GOOSE

gosling

BEAR

62

SHEEP

lamb

BUTTERFLY

caterpillar

DOG

puppy

DUCK   duckling

fawn

HEN

DEER

chick   63

THE LITTLEST
CHILDREN

big brother

mother

baby

teething ring

baby carriage

baby powder

baby bath

playpen

diaper

64

crib

father

big sister

rag doll

ttle

chair

bottle

baby lotion

teething toast

harness

toddler

cradle

cloth book

65

PARTS OF THE BODY

head for thinking

ears for listening

eyes for seeing

nose for breathing and smelling

mouth for eating and talking

neck to hold head up

tongue for tasting

teeth for biting and chewing

shoulders for carrying

chest for breathing

back for lying on

arms for pushing

and pulling

hands for holding

tail for wagging

(Don't worry if you don't have one.)

feet for walking

COOKING AND BAKING

Thumper and his brothers and sisters love to help in the kitchen when it's Mother Rabbit's baking day. There are lots of bowls to scrape out and delicious smells coming from the oven.

vinegar

rack

blender

stove

salt shaker

ladle

fau[c]

saucepan

oil

sink

fish

soup pot

platter

oven

potato

sto[

cupboard

spilled milk

cloth

apron

mixing bow[l]

can opener

washing machine

eggshells

kettle

coffeepot

scale

ty dishes

refrigerator

egg
beater

meat

door

wooden spoon

doormat

colander

cabbage   onions
carrots

gelatin

lemon

tomatoes

lettuce

pepper mill
ugar

cookbook

cupcakes

our

able

69

AT THE MARKET

vegetable counter

cucumber

customer

grocer

scale

potatoes

tomatoes

onions

lettuce

watermelon

asparagus

cabbage

carrots

cauliflower

brussels sprouts

green beans

peppers

eggplant

fruit counter

artichoke

bananas

oranges

grapes

pears

peaches

melons

money

pineapple

grocer

customer

gooseberries

pomegranates

raspberries

lemons

strawberries

apple

candy

grocer

crackers

eggs

FRESH EGGS

customer

bread

tea

flour

TEA TEA

FLOUR

jam

JAM

honey

shrimp

cheese

duck

butter

SUGAR

sugar

herring

turkey

SOAP POWDER

soap powder

flounder

bacon

POLISH

polish

lobster

broom

kitten who wanted the apple at the bottom of the pile

trash

AT THE DEPARTMENT STORE

MATERIALS and NOTIONS

buttons

buckles

thread

counter

thimbles

zippers

trimmings

saleswoman

perfume

talcum powder

bath salt

lipsticks

razors

face cream

customer

change purses

scarves

belts

gloves

handbags

wallets

bracelets

necklace

pins

ring

floorwalker

electric drill

curtain rod

doorknobs

glue

GLUE

paint

tiles

wood

ELEVATOR

delivery truck

store detective

elevator

elevator operator

manager

73

BUYING CLOTHES

Mrs. Mouse takes all her children out to buy them new clothes.

Here are all the clothes they try on.

shirt

trousers

parka

slip

dress

skirt

tights

jacket

undershirt

underpants

booties

slippers

socks

sandals

coat

sweater

shoes

mittens

boots

hat

scarf

bonnet

blanket

nightgown

hat

cap

blouse

tie

blazer

jumper

shorts

striped socks

tape measure

shoes

shoe lace

pin cushion

(This should be
tied in a bow.)

bookbag

Here are
some clothes that didn't fit.

75

TOYS

fort

pedal car

toy soldier

train

magic set

tracks

model plane

doll house

tricycle

rocking horse

scooter

checkers

doll carriage

roller skates

kite

spinning top

rocket

ball

racing car

bus

tow truck

building blocks

baking set

77

WHAT TO DO ON A SUNNY DAY

play ball

play leapfrog

run a race

climb a tree

sail a boat

kite

have a swing

fly a kite

80

WHAT TO DO ON A RAINY DAY

muddy face

raincoat

splash in puddles

boots

write a letter

81

easel

read a book

brush

paints

paint a picture

tidy up

cowboy

dress up

nurse

bake a cake

pipe

blow bubbles

ball

play a game

THE WAY
WE FEEL

happy

thoughtful

thirsty

sad

full

hungry

ill

well

shy

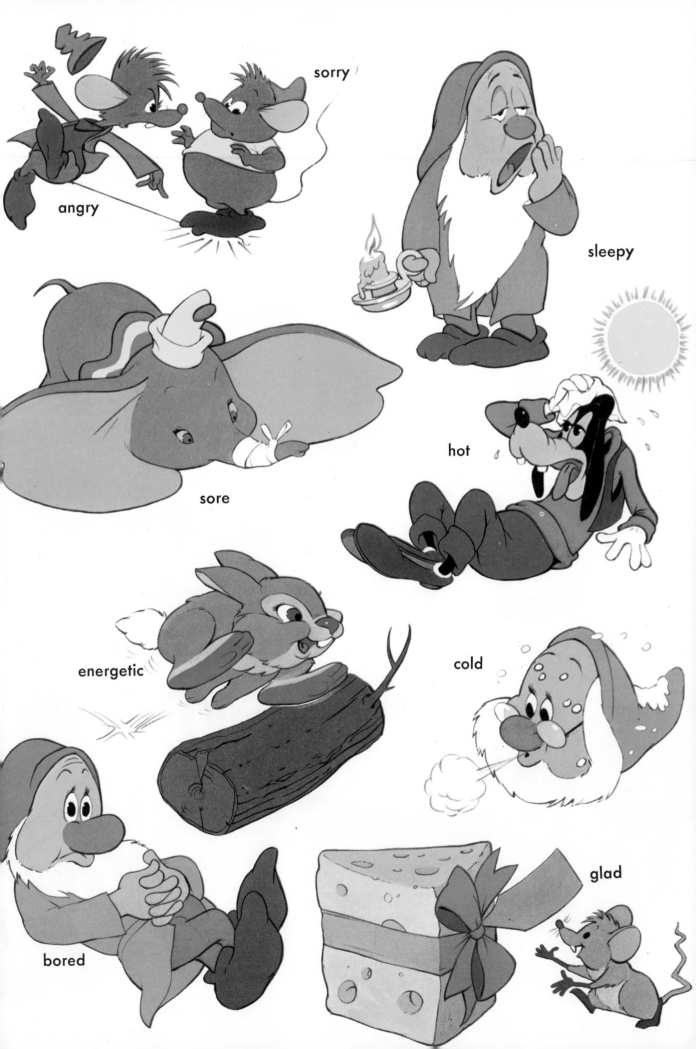

angry

sorry

sleepy

sore

hot

energetic

cold

bored

glad

MAKING THINGS

CARDBOARD BOX

garage

space helmet

hat

KNITTIN
NEEDLES

YARN

socks

scar

HAMMER

NAILS

doll house

PIECE OF
WOOD

SAW   stool

airplane

doll table

BLOCKS

SPOOL OF THR

doll's dress

tower

train station

rag doll

apron

bridge

NEEDLE

CLOTH

MODELING CLAY

paper chain

raffe

ducks

snake

mask

paper
hat

SCISSORS

PAPER

TAPE

PASTE

mosaic

a picture of mommy

paper airplane

PAINTBOX

WATER JAR

picture

BRUSHES

JARS OF PAINT

87

WHEN WE ARE SICK

cray

Pooh isn't feeling very well, and that makes him feel
a little sorry for himself. Maybe you've felt the
same way when you were sick. The doctor and nurse
will soon make Pooh better, and in the meantime,
his friends have come to cheer him up.

Dr. Owl

thermometer

stethoscope

Winnie the Pooh

spotty face

grapes

sore throat

tissues

small pot
of honey

nice warm quilt

slippers

Nurse Kanga

games

storybook

cards

coloring book

re are some things
eep Pooh happy
il he is well again.

toy train

writing
paper

envelope

visitors

scissors

bandage

pills

doctor's
bag

tweezers

spoon

cotton swabs

cough syrup

tongue depressor

flashlight

89

AT THE RAILROAD STATION

CANDY

BOOKS

candy shop

book s...

passenger car

engine

engineer

MAIL
MAIL
MAIL

picnic hamper

suitcases

parcel

mail sacks

railroad ticket

bucket

shovel

ticket collector

RESTAURANT

NOTICES

waiting room

restaurant

dining car

station master

waiter

trunk

whistle

porter

flag

baggage truck

conductor

taxi

family going on vacation

TAXI

OUT IN THE COUNTRY

owl taking a nap

acorn

caterpillar

stinging nettle
(Don't pick these.)

cattails

wagtail

primrose

ant

moss

dragonfly

wild duck

sand martin

duckweed

water vole

pond

frog

fish

squirrel

bark

woodpecker

magpie

oak tree

pinks

ivy

buttercup

fieldmouse

thrush

beetle

grasshopper

roots

seeds

bulb

mole

worm

centipede

93

tractor

field

silo

tree

fence

haystack

gate

er's wife

cow

dog

grass

horse

hen

drinking trough

henhouse

rooster

chickens

95

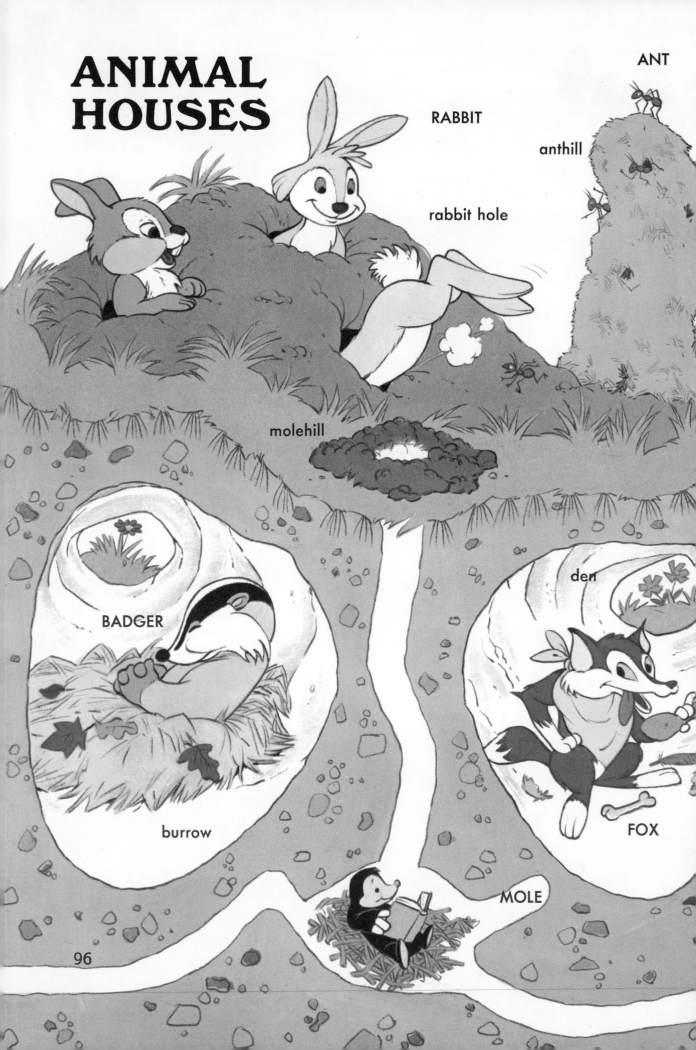

ANIMAL HOUSES

ANT

RABBIT

anthill

rabbit hole

molehill

den

BADGER

FOX

burrow

MOLE

96

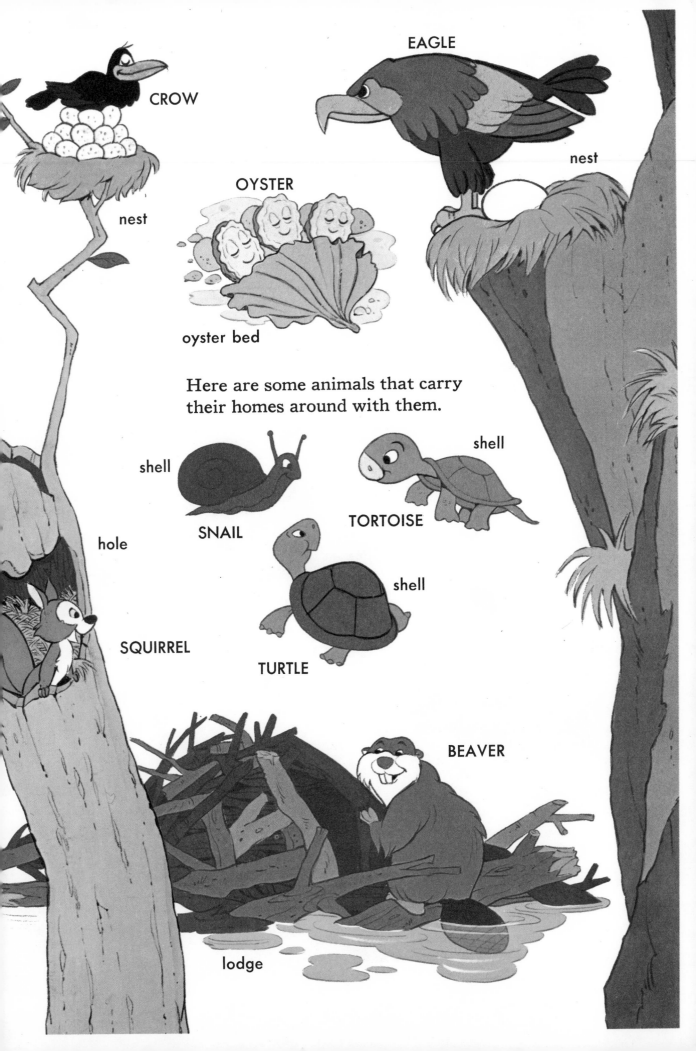

CROW

nest

EAGLE

nest

OYSTER

oyster bed

Here are some animals that carry their homes around with them.

shell

SNAIL

shell

TORTOISE

shell

TURTLE

hole

SQUIRREL

BEAVER

lodge

AT THE SEASHORE

Everybody likes to go to the seashore.
See what a big sandcastle Little Mouse is building.
Could you build one as big as that?

lighth[ouse]

fisherman

fishing line

fishing rod

fish net

bait

jetty

oar

rowboat

lobster pot

lobste[r]

crab

shrimp

sea urchin

seagull

flag

ice cream stand

ICE CREAM

beach ball

rock pool

seaweed

beach chair

sand between the toes

ice cream

rider

sandcastle

shovel

donkey

hole in the sand

sea shell

Chipmunk has dug a very deep hole.
That's why you can't see him.

99

DINING OUT

Sometimes we all go out for a meal.
Have you ever been to a restaurant like this?

cashier

bottle of wine

tray

ice water

napkin

soft drink

waiter

headwaiter

menu

punch

wine list

wine glass

Here are some good things the chef has made for you.

soup

melon

grapefruit

salmon

fish in cream sauce

roast chicken

roast leg of lamb

chef

spaghetti

steak

baked potatoes

asparagus

spinach
(very good for you)

salad

strawberry ice cream

apple pie

cream

IN

OUT

kitchen door

the bill

(Somebody has to pay.)

101

A TRIP DOWN THE RIVER

lighthouse

sea

oil tanker

buoy

captain

wheel

compass

reeds

houseboat

smokestack

pleasure boat

happy passengers

binocu

cabin

an

porthole

102

swans

crane

stately home

cargo ship

docks

bridge

boathouse

dock

treasure island

lock keeper's cottage

a boat made into a house

lock keeper

handle to wind open gate

lock gates

ropes

toll booth

103

UNDER THE SEA

boat

dolphin

mackerel

wreck

whale

coral

squid

oyster

pearl

sea anemone

lobster

104

fishing rod

bottle with
cricket

bottle with message

swordfish

diver

air bubbles

school of fish

hermit crab

deep-sea diver

old shoe

starfish

seaweed

105

jet plane

glider

helicopter

stork

THINGS THAT FLY

Isn't it nice to fly in the sky?
We can fly in an airplane, but there
are lots of things that can fly
all by themselves.

butterfly

dragonfly

very small gnat

bee

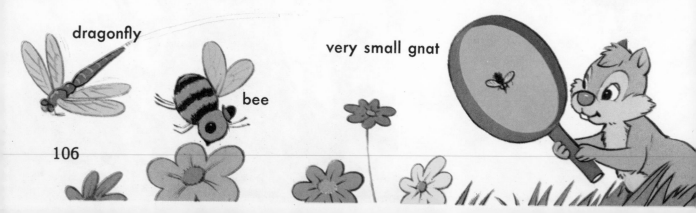

elephant
(not all elephants, only this one)

owl

crow

maple tree seed

balloon

arrow

paper airplane

bat

dandelion seeds

AT THE AIRPORT

airport bus

airline van

departure board

FLIGHT No	DESTINATION	DEP. TIME
6321	NEW YORK	08·26
6335	SIDNEY	09·12

busy road

airport terminal

MAGAZINES

check-in desk

newsstand

passenger

windsock

baggage being weighed

fuel truck

baggage truck

plane arriving

landing lights

control tower

small plane

plane taking off

airport

runway

customs

passengers

mechanic

pilot

tail

t plane

fuselage

steward

wing

624

ggage
mpartment

jet
engine

stewardess

passengers

109

SPACESHIPS

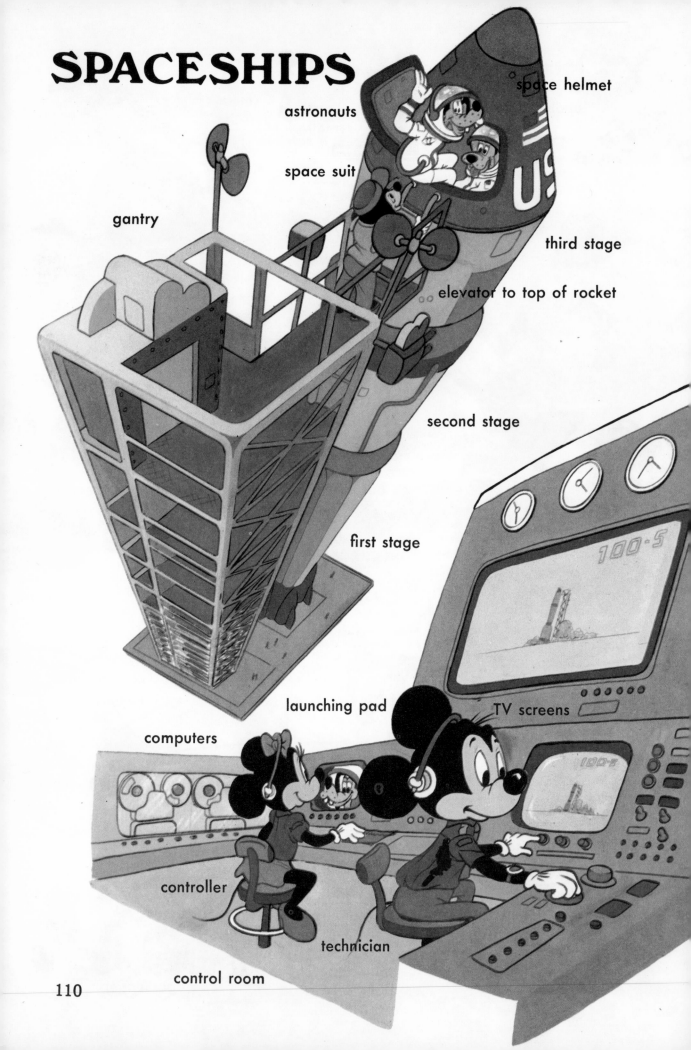

astronauts

space helmet

space suit

gantry

third stage

elevator to top of rocket

second stage

first stage

launching pad

TV screens

computers

controller

technician

control room

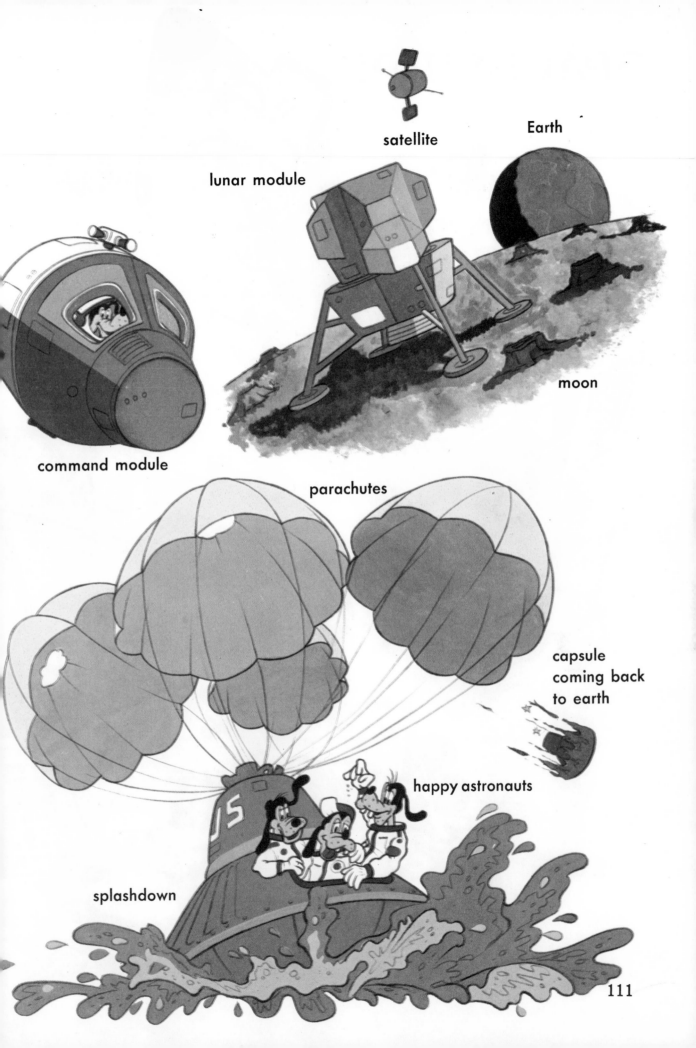

satellite

Earth

lunar module

moon

command module

parachutes

capsule coming back to earth

happy astronauts

splashdown

111

THINGS ON WHEELS

trailer

caterpillar tractor

go-cart

caravan

crane

police car

tricycle

steamroller

bicycle

van

ambulance

sports car

horse trailer

113

ALL OVER THE WORLD

Here are some people from a number of different countries. You can tell which country they belong to by the clothes they are wearing.

turban

INDIA

fez

camel

EGYPT

wooden shoes

HOLLAND

sombrero

sarape

MEXICO

parka

LAPLAND

bowler hat

umbrella

spats

ENGLAND

kimono

JAPAN

Here are some houses
and buildings from
different countries.
Can you tell which of the
people and which of the
buildings belong to the
same country?

thatched cottage

pyramid

windmill

igloo

pagoda

adobe hut

temple

MERRY-GO-ROUND

candy apple seller

sticky little bear

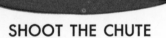

mat

SHOOT THE CHUTE

a good thrower

a bad thrower

Can you guess what little chipmunk found?

LUCKY DIP

FORTUNE
TELLER

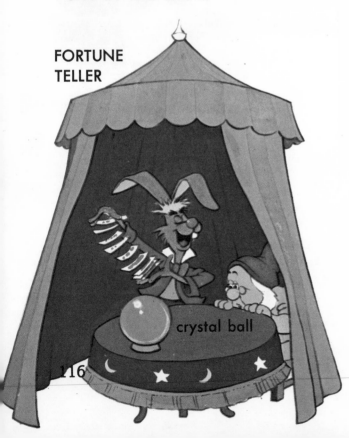

crystal ball

ROLLER COASTER

bad driver

DODGE 'EM CARS

FUN HOUSE

balloon seller

SS 'EM

nervous
little bear

COTTON CANDY STALL

target

another sticky
little bear

COTTON
CANDY

117

RIFLE RANGE

PLAY-TIME

horse chestnut

CONKERS

spinning top

see-saw

MARBLES

sandbox

SWINGING

swing

JUMPING R

bat

118

ROLLER SKATING

BASEBALL

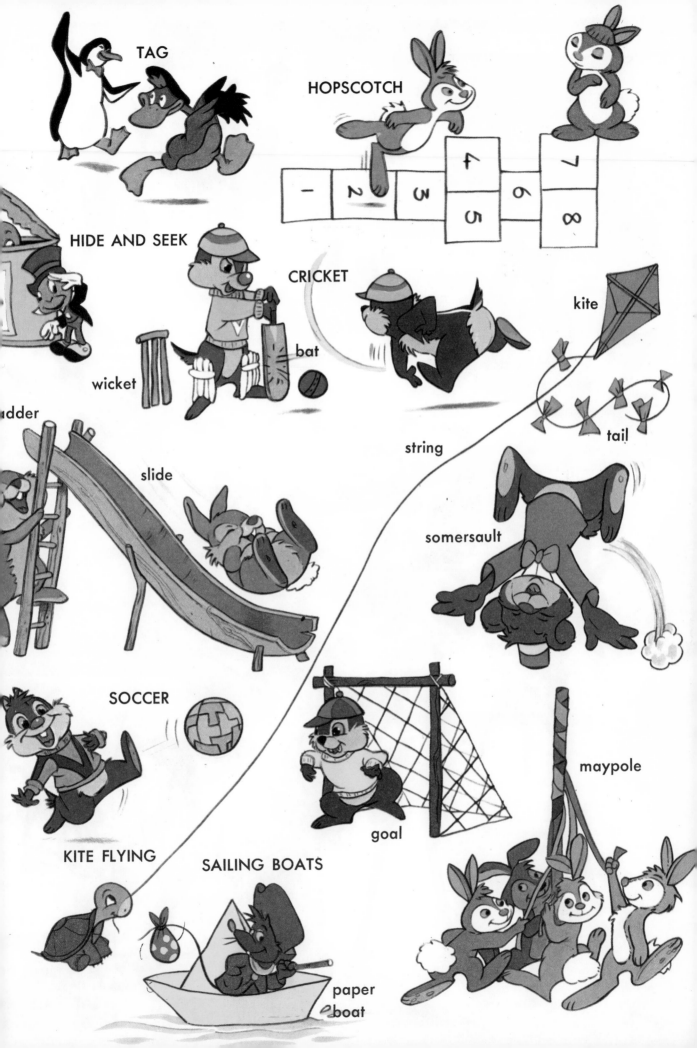

TAG

HOPSCOTCH

| 1 | 2 | 3 | 4 | 7 |
| | | | 5 | 6 | 8 |

HIDE AND SEEK

CRICKET

kite

wicket

bat

ladder

slide

string

tail

somersault

SOCCER

goal

maypole

KITE FLYING

SAILING BOATS

paper boat

wolf

deer

camel

panda

zoo keeper

AT THE ZOO

bird cage

THE CHILDREN'S ZOO

crow

rabbits

vulture

lamb

bra

lion and cub

buffalo

meat

crocodile

elephant

baby elephant

ape

tiger

tiger cub

bird

giraffe

121

AT THE TELEVISION STUDIO

floodlight

cameraman

lenses

camera

sound effects man

producer

boom

microphone

cable

spotlight

floor manager

assistants

122

set

make-up girl

star

handsome actor

pretty actress

control room

scriptwriter

script

123

AT THE FIREHOUSE

FIREHOUSE

alarm bell

fireman waiting
for a fire

helmets

coats

boots

fire pole
(for sliding down)

stairs
(for walking up)

ladder

hose

office

fire engine

brave fireman

breathing
apparatus

hatchet

telephone

desk

124

THINGS FIREMEN DO

rescue a kitten

rescue a silly boy

put out big fires

and little ones

AT THE THEATER

cherub

set

scenery

fairy godmother

box

prompter

usher

comedian

stage

curtains

audience

drink seller

seats

scene painter

scene shifter

chorus line

singer

child star

dancer

wicked villain

star
of show

127

BUILDINGS

Everybody lives in some kind of house. Is the sort
of house you live in shown here? Somewhere in the
picture are the people making this book.
Can you find them?

cottage

palace

library

lighthouse

church

town hall

art gallery

very old house

very new house

country house

town house

castle

production manager

editor

GOLDEN PRESS PUBLISHERS OF GOOD BOOKS

office building

starving artist

famous author

BUILDING A HOUSE

cement mixer

surveyor

surveyor's level

foundation

brick hod

cement bags

sand

wheelbarrow

hod carrier

carpenter's level

brick layer

mortar

pipes

door frame

plaster

plasterer

window frame

plumber

bricks

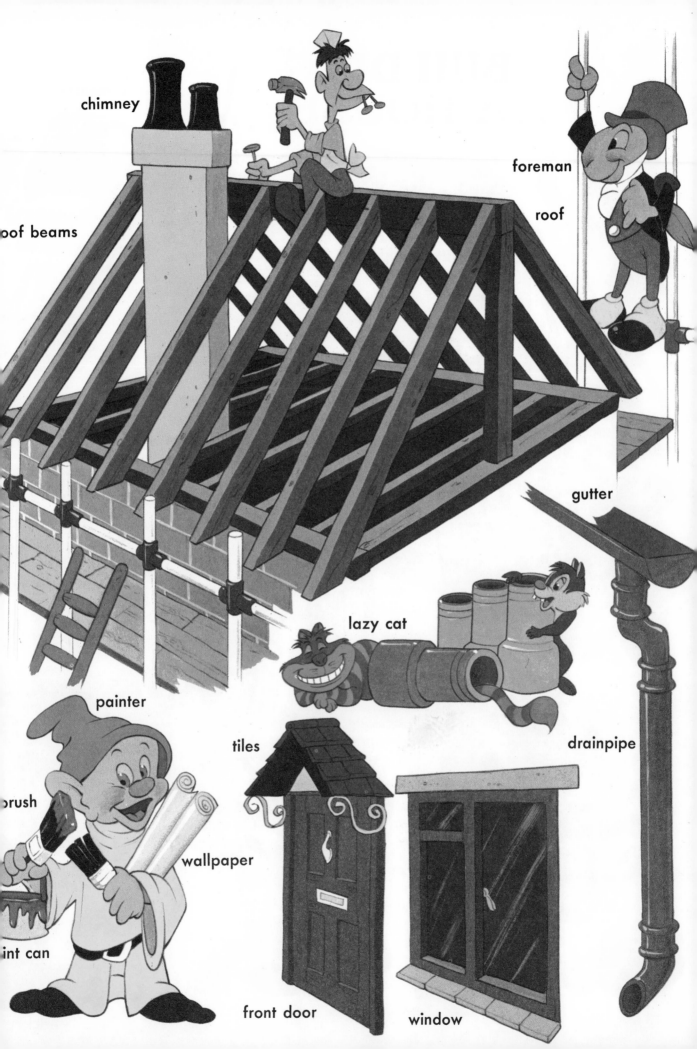

chimney

foreman

roof beams

roof

gutter

lazy cat

drainpipe

painter

tiles

brush

wallpaper

paint can

front door

window

FURNITURE

grandfather clock

plates

mug

very best teapot

cupboard

picture

vase

daffodi

corner cupboard

cushion

armchair

chair

television

high chair

desk

lamp

table

wastepaper basket

132

chest of drawers

piglet who
lost his socks

wardrobe

dressing table

bed

linen chest

record player

cradle

telephone

bookshelves

radio

couch

133

PARTY TIMES

BIRTHDAY PARTY

candles

birthday cake

pres[ents]

sandwiches

gelatin

wieners

popco[rn]

balloons

CHRISTMAS

paper hats

angel

candles

roast turkey

snappers

Christmas pudding

Christmas tree

toy sack

Santa Claus

reindeer

sleigh

stocking

lots of presents

EASTER

Easter egg

hot cross bun

chocolate bunny

chick

HALLOWEEN

o' lantern

broomstick

witch

witch's cat

dunking for apples

mask

FOURTH OF JULY

rocket

being careful

fireworks

sparkler

bonfire

firecracker

135

AT THE CIRCUS

audience

strong man

ringmaster

acrobat

clever rider

trapeze artist

one-man band

clown

bareback rider

unicycle

dancing horse

popcorn

popcorn seller

cage

tightrope walker

lion

ladder

balancing
pole

whip

lion tamer

tightrope

top hat

performing seal

dancing elephant

hoop

circus band

forming dog

BATHTIME

sponge

soap

soap dish

soap bubbles

warm water

boat

bathtub

back brush

bath mat

gauze

toothbrushes

toothpaste

glass

bandage

cotton

medicine cabinet
(not for children)

towel rack

towel

bathrobe

shower

shower cap

faucets

washcloth

slippers

sink

talcum powder

clean ears

ready for bed

clean neck

nice clean teeth

139

BEDTIME

ceiling

moon

bat

picture frame

window

picture

It's time for little chipmunks to be in bed. One good little chipmunk is all ready to go to sleep, but the other little chipmunk is wide awake.

apple

headboard

bed

pillow

sheet

bedside table

pipe

fat

patchwork quilt

slippers

favorite toy

140

picture book

curtains

door

wallpaper

clock

night light

mother

storybook

carpet

141